Printed in Great Britain
by Amazon

62444241R00071